DIRECTOR´S Notebook kids

Story Film House Books ©
DIRECTOR´S NOTEBOOK KIDS (CINEMA ARTISTS COLLECTION)
Published by Story Film House™
Story Film House (Bogota – Los Angeles)
(571)3033081 (57)3012794409 – (1) 4242530441

Printed in USA. / Impreso en USA
by Create Space.
First edition Published by Story Film House.
www.StoryFilmHouse.com / www.CinemaNotebooks.com

NAME

CONTACT NUMBER

SPECIAL INFO

1) QUICK STUDY

Learn the basics

COLOR IT

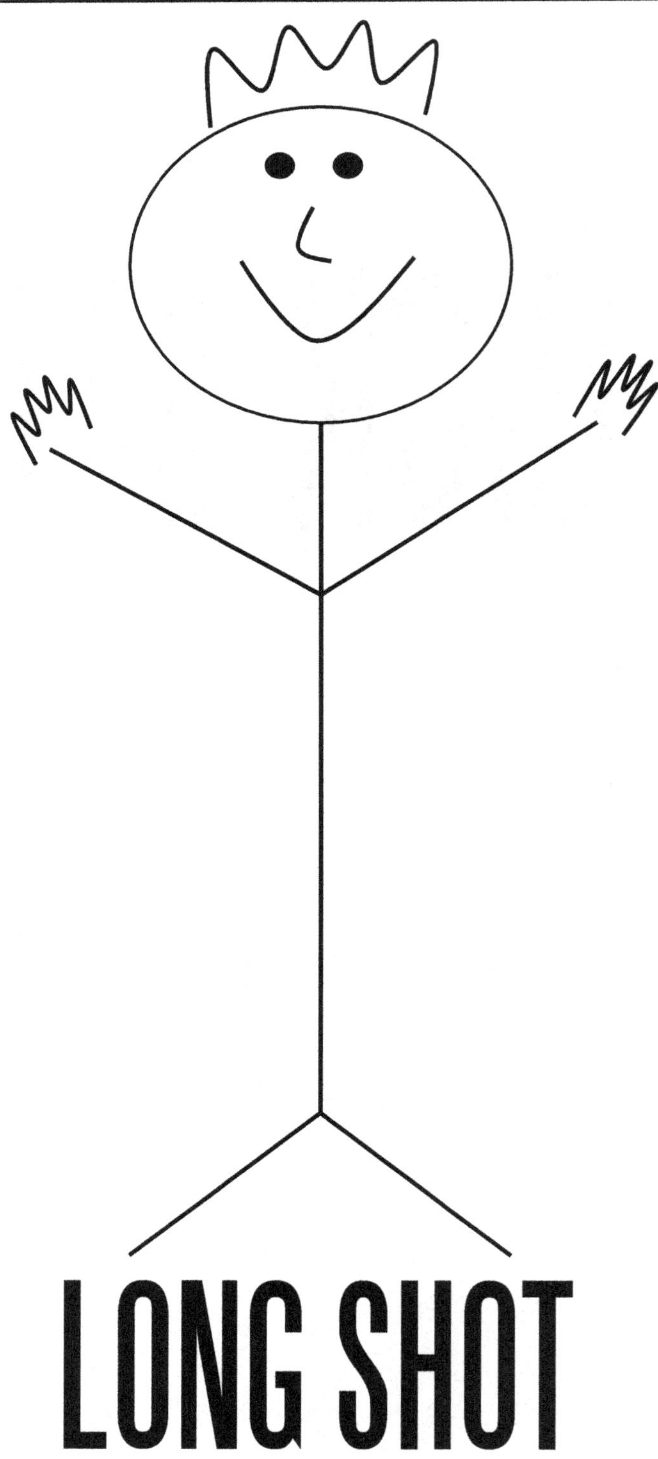

LONG SHOT

COLOR IT

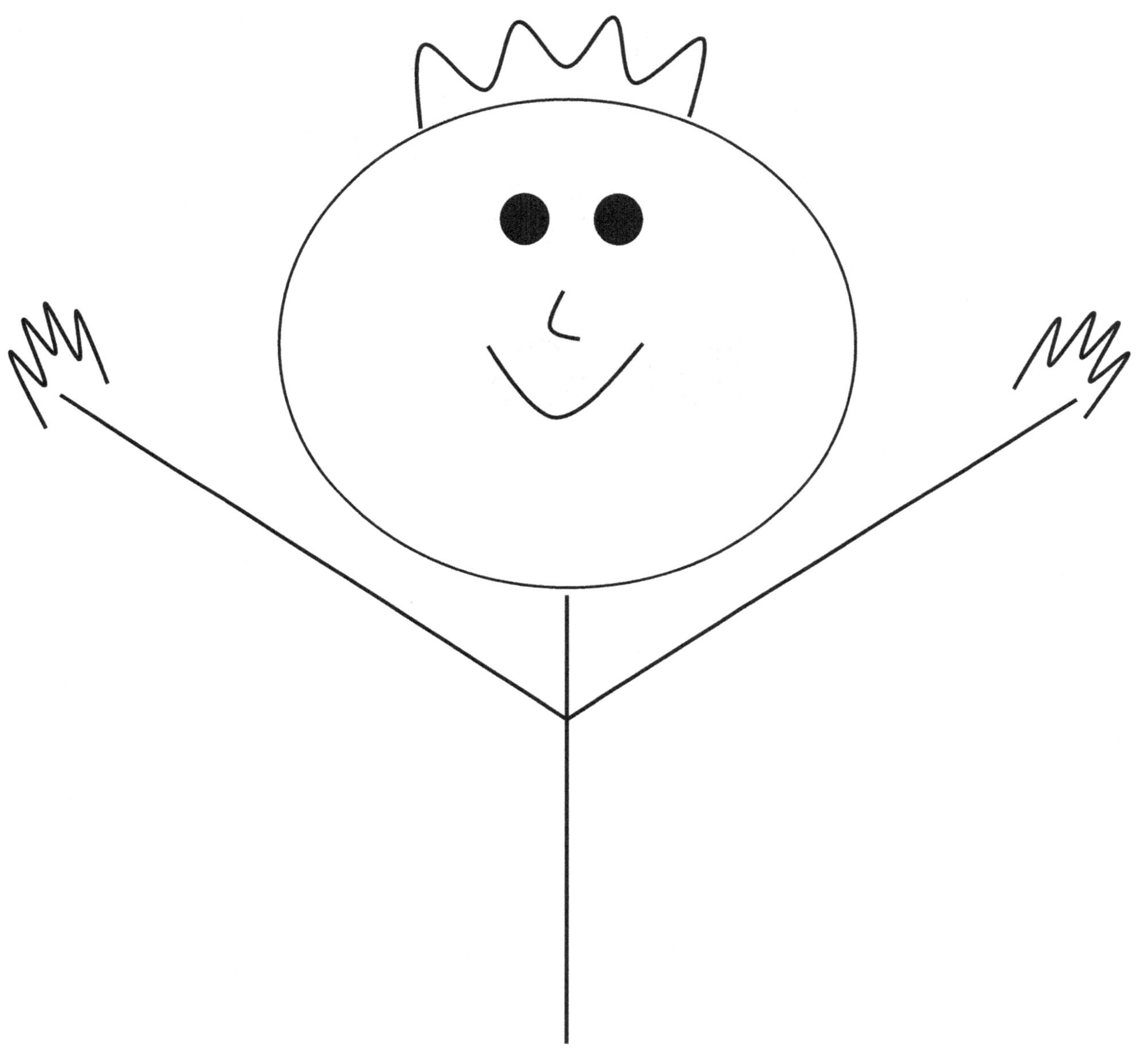

MEDIUM SHOT

COLOR IT

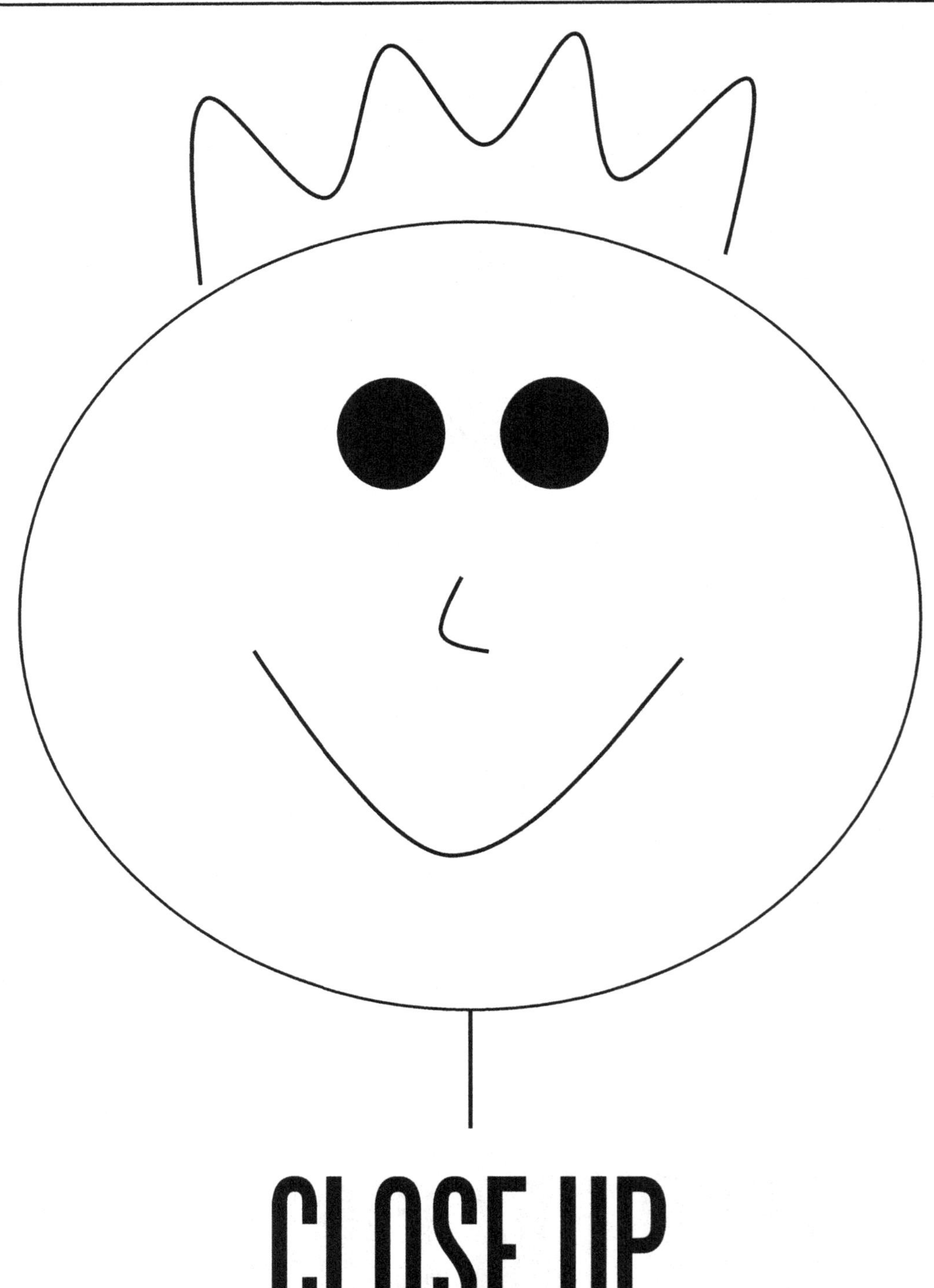

CLOSE UP

DRAW OR CUT A PICTURE

DIRECTORS WORK MAKING...

MOVIES

TELEVISION SERIES

MUSICALS

THEATRE PLAYS

DRAW OR CUT A PICTURE

DIRECTORS WORK MAKING...

MUSIC VIDEOS

TV COMMERCIALS

CIRCUS SHOWS

ON AIR TV

GAMES

Let’s play a game

WHAT DO YOU NEED TO MAKE A MOVIE

A	C	P	M	D	Z	A	D	R	E
S	A	P	R	O	D	U	C	E	R
Y	M	E	D	I	T	O	R	X	C
T	E	D	I	R	E	C	T	O	R
O	R	G	Q	N	F	W	R	L	E
K	A	H	A	C	T	O	R	S	W
J	I	L	I	G	H	T	S	B	G
S	C	R	E	E	N	P	L	A	Y

CAMERA
SCREENPLAY
ACTORS
PRODUCER
DIRECTOR
CREW
LIGHTS
EDITOR

CAMERA MOVEMENTS

A	R	J	T	E	M	P	O	Y	J
N	S	T	I	L	T	U	P	Z	U
I	N	G	W	E	T	F	A	U	H
Y	C	X	K	B	J	I	N	C	A
L	V	T	I	L	T	D	O	W	N
L	M	D	Q	A	L	R	B	I	P
O	P	E	D	E	S	T	A	L	A
D	O	L	L	Y	O	U	T	C	P

TILTUP
TILTDOWN
DOLLYIN
DOLLYOUT
PEDESTAL
PAN

SHOTS

M	E	D	I	U	M	S	H	O	T
C	L	O	S	E	U	P	I	A	O
A	O	U	E	W	C	C	Y	Z	H
K	N	T	S	V	E	E	E	L	S
U	G	X	H	F	N	D	G	J	G
B	S	A	M	E	R	I	C	A	N
Q	H	K	R	U	O	C	M	P	O
J	O	A	M	E	R	I	C	A	L

LONGSHOT
MEDIUMSHOT
CLOSEUP
ECU (EXTREME CLOSEUP)
AMERICAN
ELS (EXTREME LONG SHOT)

MOST IMPORTANT FESTIVALS AND AWARDS

B	A	C	W	S	N	O	V	Z	T
E	F	A	Y	U	D	S	E	F	O
R	I	N	G	N	K	C	L	M	R
L	F	N	A	D	J	A	U	G	O
I	E	E	C	A	I	R	H	W	N
N	S	S	R	N	I	Z	O	K	T
R	T	Q	Z	C	W	P	O	R	O
B	S	A	T	E	G	T	H	T	B

CANNES
OSCAR
SUNDANCE
BERLIN
AFIFEST
TORONTO

DIRECTORS WORK MAKING

M	A	S	X	F	Y	E	P	R	O
U	D	F	I	L	M	S	G	H	N
S	T	V	S	E	R	I	E	S	A
I	J	C	I	K	B	Q	F	Z	I
C	I	R	C	U	S	P	U	S	R
A	H	F	E	R	T	A	E	H	T
L	M	V	T	Y	A	B	T	O	V
S	W	O	H	S	V	V	R	S	W

FILMS
THEATRE
TVSERIES
TVSHOWS
MUSICALS
ON AIR TV
CIRCUS

WATCH A MOVIE AND PRESS PAUSE AT ANY TIME.
DRAW WHAT YOU SEE AND SELECT TYPE OF SHOT

TITLE:

LONG SHOT

MEDIUM SHOT

CLOSE UP

WATCH A MOVIE AND PRESS PAUSE AT ANY TIME.
DRAW WHAT YOU SEE AND SELECT TYPE OF SHOT

TITLE:

LONG SHOT

MEDIUM SHOT

CLOSE UP

WATCH A MOVIE AND PRESS PAUSE AT ANY TIME.
DRAW WHAT YOU SEE AND SELECT TYPE OF SHOT

TITLE:

LONG SHOT

MEDIUM SHOT

CLOSE UP

WATCH A MOVIE AND PRESS PAUSE AT ANY TIME.
DRAW WHAT YOU SEE AND SELECT TYPE OF SHOT

TITLE:

LONG SHOT

MEDIUM SHOT

CLOSE UP

WATCH A MOVIE AND PRESS PAUSE AT ANY TIME.
DRAW WHAT YOU SEE AND SELECT TYPE OF SHOT

TITLE:

LONG SHOT

MEDIUM SHOT

CLOSE UP

WATCH A MOVIE AND PRESS PAUSE AT ANY TIME.
DRAW WHAT YOU SEE AND SELECT TYPE OF SHOT

TITLE:

LONG SHOT

MEDIUM SHOT

CLOSE UP

WATCH A MOVIE AND PRESS PAUSE AT ANY TIME.
DRAW WHAT YOU SEE AND SELECT TYPE OF SHOT

TITLE:

LONG SHOT

MEDIUM SHOT

CLOSE UP

WATCH A MOVIE AND PRESS PAUSE AT ANY TIME.
DRAW WHAT YOU SEE AND SELECT TYPE OF SHOT

TITLE:

LONG SHOT

MEDIUM SHOT

CLOSE UP

WATCH A MOVIE AND PRESS PAUSE AT ANY TIME.
DRAW WHAT YOU SEE AND SELECT TYPE OF SHOT

TITLE:

LONG SHOT

MEDIUM SHOT

CLOSE UP

WATCH A MOVIE AND PRESS PAUSE AT ANY TIME.
DRAW WHAT YOU SEE AND SELECT TYPE OF SHOT

TITLE:

LONG SHOT

MEDIUM SHOT

CLOSE UP

CREATE SHOTS

Work as a professional director and create a shot

CREATE YOUR OWN SHOTS

TITLE:

LONG SHOT

MEDIUM SHOT

CLOSE UP

CREATE YOUR OWN SHOTS

TITLE:

LONG SHOT

MEDIUM SHOT

CLOSE UP

CREATE YOUR OWN SHOTS

TITLE:

LONG SHOT

MEDIUM SHOT

CLOSE UP

CREATE YOUR OWN SHOTS

TITLE:

LONG SHOT

MEDIUM SHOT

CLOSE UP

CREATE YOUR OWN SHOTS

TITLE:

LONG SHOT

MEDIUM SHOT

CLOSE UP

CREATE YOUR OWN SHOTS

TITLE:

LONG SHOT

MEDIUM SHOT

CLOSE UP

CREATE YOUR OWN SHOTS

TITLE:

LONG SHOT

MEDIUM SHOT

CLOSE UP

CREATE YOUR OWN SHOTS

TITLE:

LONG SHOT

MEDIUM SHOT

CLOSE UP

CREATE YOUR OWN SHOTS

TITLE:

LONG SHOT

MEDIUM SHOT

CLOSE UP

CREATE YOUR OWN SHOTS

TITLE:

LONG SHOT

MEDIUM SHOT

CLOSE UP

CREATE YOUR OWN SHOTS

TITLE:

LONG SHOT

MEDIUM SHOT

CLOSE UP

CREATE YOUR OWN SHOTS

TITLE:

LONG SHOT

MEDIUM SHOT

CLOSE UP

CREATE YOUR OWN SHOTS

TITLE:

LONG SHOT

MEDIUM SHOT

CLOSE UP

JOURNEY PLANNER

Plan your journey

DAY ______

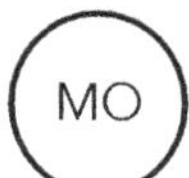

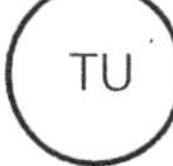

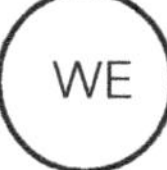

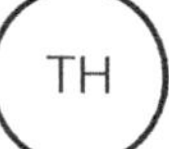

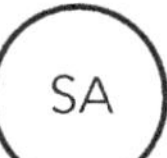

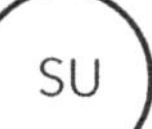

TO DO

TO STUDY

QUOTES / MOVIES / BOOKS / IDEAS

FRIENDS

ONLY FOR ME

DAY ______

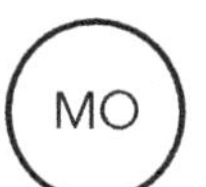

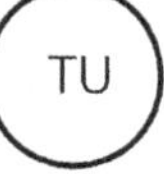

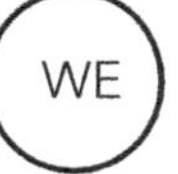

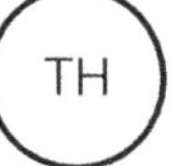

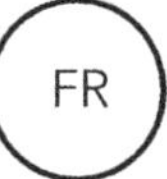

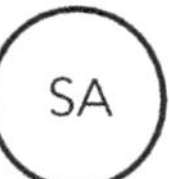

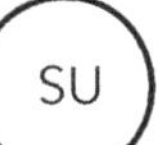

TO DO	TO STUDY

QUOTES / MOVIES / BOOKS / IDEAS

FRIENDS	ONLY FOR ME

DAY ______

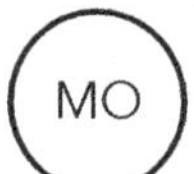

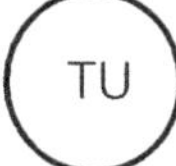

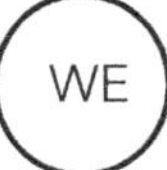

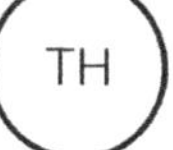

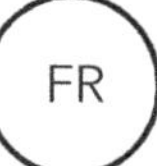

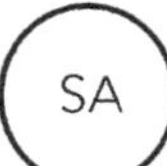

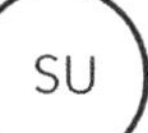

TO DO

TO STUDY

QUOTES / MOVIES / BOOKS / IDEAS

FRIENDS

ONLY FOR ME

DAY ______

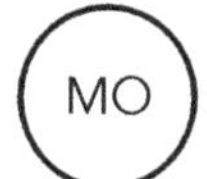

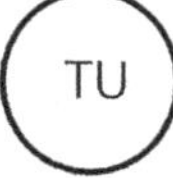

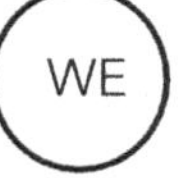

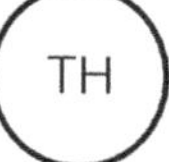

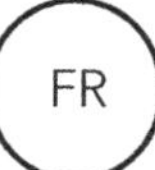

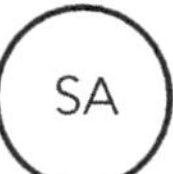

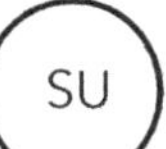

TO DO	TO STUDY

QUOTES / MOVIES / BOOKS / IDEAS

FRIENDS	ONLY FOR ME

DAY ______

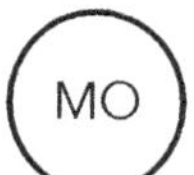

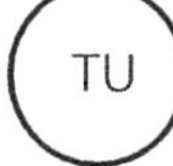

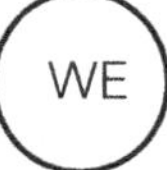

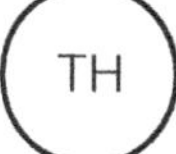

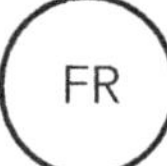

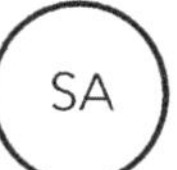

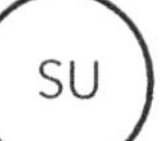

TO DO	TO STUDY

QUOTES / MOVIES / BOOKS / IDEAS

FRIENDS	ONLY FOR ME

DAY ______

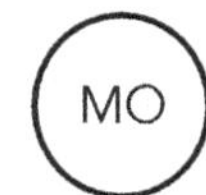

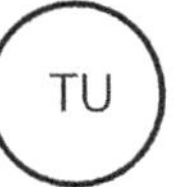

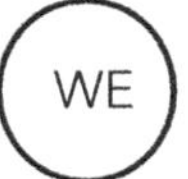

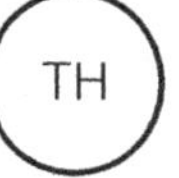

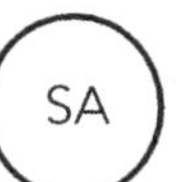

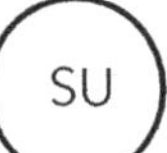

TO DO	TO STUDY

QUOTES / MOVIES / BOOKS / IDEAS

FRIENDS	ONLY FOR ME

DAY ______

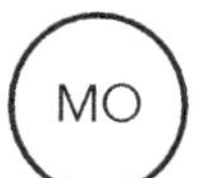

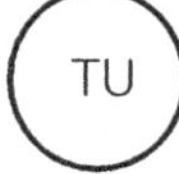

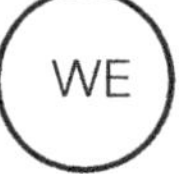

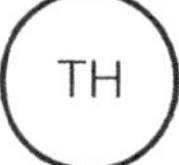

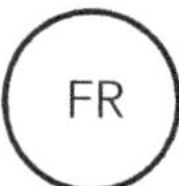

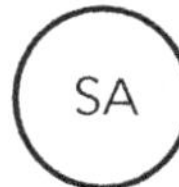

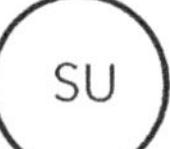

TO DO	TO STUDY

QUOTES / MOVIES / BOOKS / IDEAS

FRIENDS	ONLY FOR ME

DAY ______

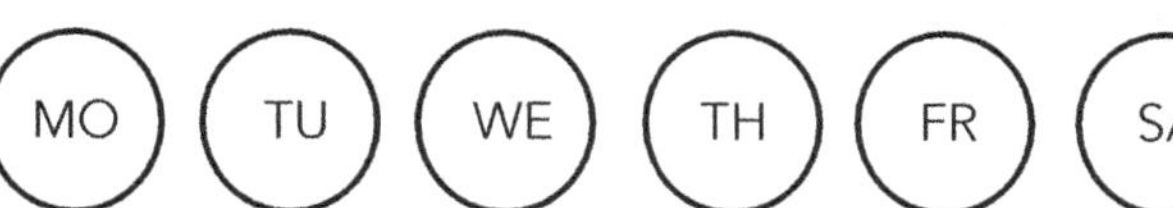

TO DO	TO STUDY

QUOTES / MOVIES / BOOKS / IDEAS

FRIENDS	ONLY FOR ME

DAY ______

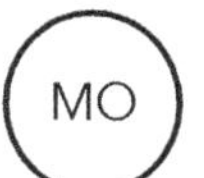

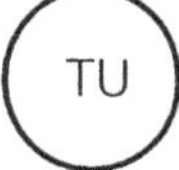

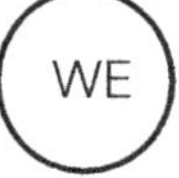

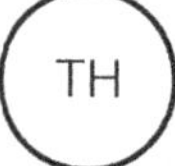

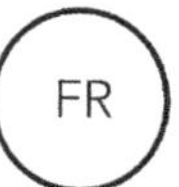

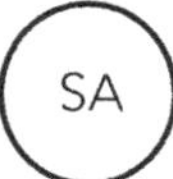

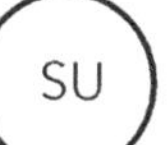

TO DO

TO STUDY

QUOTES / MOVIES / BOOKS / IDEAS

FRIENDS

ONLY FOR ME

DAY ______

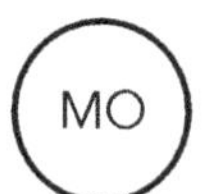

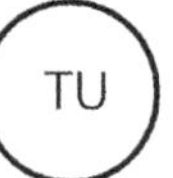

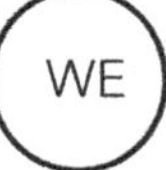

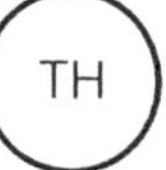

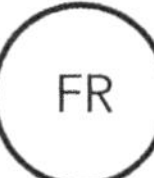

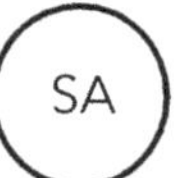

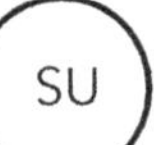

TO DO

TO STUDY

QUOTES / MOVIES / BOOKS / IDEAS

FRIENDS

ONLY FOR ME

WRITE A STORY

Everything you need to write a story.

FILM CREDITS

Create your own credits of the movies you have seen.

MOVIE TITLE
DIRECTED BY:
PRODUCED BY:
DIRECTOR OF PHOTOGRAPHY:
PRODUCTION DESIGNER:
ACTORS:
EXECUTIVE PRODUCERS:
MUSIC BY:
COSTUME DESIGNER:
EDITED BY:
SCREENPLAY BY:
CASTING BY:

MOVIE TITLE
DIRECTED BY:
PRODUCED BY:
DIRECTOR OF PHOTOGRAPHY:
PRODUCTION DESIGNER:
ACTORS:
EXECUTIVE PRODUCERS:
MUSIC BY:
COSTUME DESIGNER:
EDITED BY:
SCREENPLAY BY:
CASTING BY:

MOVIE TITLE
DIRECTED BY:
PRODUCED BY:
DIRECTOR OF PHOTOGRAPHY:
PRODUCTION DESIGNER:
ACTORS:
EXECUTIVE PRODUCERS:
MUSIC BY:
COSTUME DESIGNER:
EDITED BY:
SCREENPLAY BY:
CASTING BY:

MOVIE TITLE
DIRECTED BY:
PRODUCED BY:
DIRECTOR OF PHOTOGRAPHY:
PRODUCTION DESIGNER:
ACTORS:
EXECUTIVE PRODUCERS:
MUSIC BY:
COSTUME DESIGNER:
EDITED BY:
SCREENPLAY BY:
CASTING BY:

MOVIE TITLE
DIRECTED BY:
PRODUCED BY:
DIRECTOR OF PHOTOGRAPHY:
PRODUCTION DESIGNER:
ACTORS:
EXECUTIVE PRODUCERS:
MUSIC BY:
COSTUME DESIGNER:
EDITED BY:
SCREENPLAY BY:
CASTING BY:

MOVIE TITLE
DIRECTED BY:
PRODUCED BY:
DIRECTOR OF PHOTOGRAPHY:
PRODUCTION DESIGNER:
ACTORS:
EXECUTIVE PRODUCERS:
MUSIC BY:
COSTUME DESIGNER:
EDITED BY:
SCREENPLAY BY:
CASTING BY:

MOVIE TITLE
DIRECTED BY:
PRODUCED BY:
DIRECTOR OF PHOTOGRAPHY:
PRODUCTION DESIGNER:
ACTORS:
EXECUTIVE PRODUCERS:
MUSIC BY:
COSTUME DESIGNER:
EDITED BY:
SCREENPLAY BY:
CASTING BY:

MOVIE TITLE
DIRECTED BY:
PRODUCED BY:
DIRECTOR OF PHOTOGRAPHY:
PRODUCTION DESIGNER:
ACTORS:
EXECUTIVE PRODUCERS:
MUSIC BY:
COSTUME DESIGNER:
EDITED BY:
SCREENPLAY BY:
CASTING BY:

MOVIE TITLE
DIRECTED BY:
PRODUCED BY:
DIRECTOR OF PHOTOGRAPHY:
PRODUCTION DESIGNER:
ACTORS:
EXECUTIVE PRODUCERS:
MUSIC BY:
COSTUME DESIGNER:
EDITED BY:
SCREENPLAY BY:
CASTING BY:

MOVIE TITLE
DIRECTED BY:
PRODUCED BY:
DIRECTOR OF PHOTOGRAPHY:
PRODUCTION DESIGNER:
ACTORS:
EXECUTIVE PRODUCERS:
MUSIC BY:
COSTUME DESIGNER:
EDITED BY:
SCREENPLAY BY:
CASTING BY:

MOVIE TITLE
DIRECTED BY:
PRODUCED BY:
DIRECTOR OF PHOTOGRAPHY:
PRODUCTION DESIGNER:
ACTORS:
EXECUTIVE PRODUCERS:
MUSIC BY:
COSTUME DESIGNER:
EDITED BY:
SCREENPLAY BY:
CASTING BY:

MOVIE TITLE
DIRECTED BY:
PRODUCED BY:
DIRECTOR OF PHOTOGRAPHY:
PRODUCTION DESIGNER:
ACTORS:
EXECUTIVE PRODUCERS:
MUSIC BY:
COSTUME DESIGNER:
EDITED BY:
SCREENPLAY BY:
CASTING BY:

MOVIE TITLE
DIRECTED BY:
PRODUCED BY:
DIRECTOR OF PHOTOGRAPHY:
PRODUCTION DESIGNER:
ACTORS:
EXECUTIVE PRODUCERS:
MUSIC BY:
COSTUME DESIGNER:
EDITED BY:
SCREENPLAY BY:
CASTING BY:

MOVIE TITLE
DIRECTED BY:
PRODUCED BY:
DIRECTOR OF PHOTOGRAPHY:
PRODUCTION DESIGNER:
ACTORS:
EXECUTIVE PRODUCERS:
MUSIC BY:
COSTUME DESIGNER:
EDITED BY:
SCREENPLAY BY:
CASTING BY:

MOVIE TITLE
DIRECTED BY:
PRODUCED BY:
DIRECTOR OF PHOTOGRAPHY:
PRODUCTION DESIGNER:
ACTORS:
EXECUTIVE PRODUCERS:
MUSIC BY:
COSTUME DESIGNER:
EDITED BY:
SCREENPLAY BY:
CASTING BY:

MOVIE TITLE
DIRECTED BY:
PRODUCED BY:
DIRECTOR OF PHOTOGRAPHY:
PRODUCTION DESIGNER:
ACTORS:
EXECUTIVE PRODUCERS:
MUSIC BY:
COSTUME DESIGNER:
EDITED BY:
SCREENPLAY BY:
CASTING BY:

MOVIE TITLE
DIRECTED BY:
PRODUCED BY:
DIRECTOR OF PHOTOGRAPHY:
PRODUCTION DESIGNER:
ACTORS:
EXECUTIVE PRODUCERS:
MUSIC BY:
COSTUME DESIGNER:
EDITED BY:
SCREENPLAY BY:
CASTING BY:

MOVIE TITLE
DIRECTED BY:
PRODUCED BY:
DIRECTOR OF PHOTOGRAPHY:
PRODUCTION DESIGNER:
ACTORS:
EXECUTIVE PRODUCERS:
MUSIC BY:
COSTUME DESIGNER:
EDITED BY:
SCREENPLAY BY:
CASTING BY:

MOVIE TITLE
DIRECTED BY:
PRODUCED BY:
DIRECTOR OF PHOTOGRAPHY:
PRODUCTION DESIGNER:
ACTORS:
EXECUTIVE PRODUCERS:
MUSIC BY:
COSTUME DESIGNER:
EDITED BY:
SCREENPLAY BY:
CASTING BY:

MOVIE TITLE	
DIRECTED BY:	
PRODUCED BY:	
DIRECTOR OF PHOTOGRAPHY:	
PRODUCTION DESIGNER:	
ACTORS:	
EXECUTIVE PRODUCERS:	
MUSIC BY:	
COSTUME DESIGNER:	
EDITED BY:	
SCREENPLAY BY:	
CASTING BY:	

MOVIE TITLE
DIRECTED BY:
PRODUCED BY:
DIRECTOR OF PHOTOGRAPHY:
PRODUCTION DESIGNER:
ACTORS:
EXECUTIVE PRODUCERS:
MUSIC BY:
COSTUME DESIGNER:
EDITED BY:
SCREENPLAY BY:
CASTING BY:

Story Film House "Books"
www.StoryFilmHouse.com
(57-301) 279 4409

12511717R00059

Made in the USA
Monee, IL
26 September 2019